Original title:

Smoky Echoes Above the Glowing Fen

Author: Kaido Väinamäe
ISBN HARDBACK: 978-1-80559-091-0
ISBN PAPERBACK: 978-1-80559-590-8

Floating Memories Beneath the Veil

Whispers of the past do call,
Drifting through the shadows' thrall,
Fleeting echoes softly play,
In the dawn of yesterday.

Time unspools like silken thread,
Stitching stories, gently spread,
Fragments rise and softly glow,
In the twilight's tender flow.

Beneath the veil, the dreams reside,
In the stillness, hearts collide,
Moments hung in silver light,
Shimmering through the veil of night.

Each memory a fragile spark,
Lighting up the veiled dark,
Cascading through the endless blue,
Whispers of a life once true.

Floating softly, memories sigh,
Carried on the winds that fly,
In the hush of the evening breeze,
They dance among the ancient trees.

Spirit of the Sullen Marsh

In a wetland's embrace, shadows creep,
Whispers of silence, secrets to keep.
Reeds sway gently, a sorrowful dance,
Echoes of longing, a fleeting glance.

Glimmers of moonlight kiss the dark,
A haunting stillness, an ancient spark.
Nature's lament, a song that weeps,
In the sullen marsh, where the spirit sleeps.

Nightfall's Luminescent Lullaby

As dusk unfurls its velvet wings,
Stars emerge with soft, gentle sings.
Crickets strum their nightly refrain,
In a soothing lull, they ease our pain.

The world transforms with twilight's kiss,
Dreams ignite in the starlit bliss.
Moonbeams dance like whispers rare,
In nightfall's arms, we shed our care.

Enchanted Mists on Evening Waters

Misty veils cover the serene lake,
Reflections shimmer, secrets awake.
Waves cradle whispers of twilight's sigh,
Softly weaving dreams as moments fly.

In the stillness, a tender grace,
Time slows down in this sacred space.
Nature's breath, a gentle caress,
Enchanted mists weave their soft dress.

Voices of the Hidden Grove

In the heart of silence, soft voices dwell,
Echoes of stories only trees can tell.
Leaves murmur secrets in the gentle breeze,
Carrying wisdom with such sweet ease.

Roots entwine beneath earth's embrace,
Guardians of time in this hidden place.
Each rustling leaf is a tale untold,
In the grove's heart, mysteries unfold.

Solitude in the Fog-Cloaked Night

In the stillness of the night,
Fog wraps around the weary soul.
Each breath a silent whisper,
Echoes of the heart's deep toll.

Moonlight dances on the ground,
Shadows stretch and softly blend.
Solitude in silence found,
Where dreams and thoughts transcend.

Stars blink through a ghostly veil,
Guiding paths unseen by day.
The nightingale's haunting wail,
Sings of love that slipped away.

Branches sway in gentle breeze,
Caressing secrets of the past.
In this fog, the spirit sees,
Moments fleeting, yet so vast.

Time drips slow like melting ice,
Wrapped in haunting thoughts of woe.
In solitude, we pay the price,
For quietude when none can know.

Secrets of the Whirling Mist

In the heart of swirling haze,
Whispers of forgotten dreams.
Each shadow dances, softly sways,
Holding truths in silent schemes.

Misty fingers brush the ground,
Unlocking doors to realms within.
Secrets lost, now to be found,
Where the whispers weave their spin.

Figures drift and fade away,
Stories carved in twilight's hue.
In this place where spirits play,
Yearning hearts find skies anew.

The wisp of smoke, faint and light,
Carries hopes like fragile wings.
In this mist, both day and night,
The soul remembers what it sings.

Veils of time and memory blend,
As shadows move with grace untold.
Secrets whispered, never end,
In the mist, both warm and cold.

Wandering Dreams in Wistful Haze

Wandering through a world of dreams,
Where whispers float like softest sighs.
In the haze, the night redeems,
Lost moments that the heart still tries.

Stars flicker in the muted glow,
Guiding thoughts that twist and turn.
In every shadow, secrets flow,
Fueling the flame that will not burn.

Each sigh a wish upon the breeze,
Carried forth to lands unknown.
In this dreamscape, hearts find ease,
Where every ache feels just like home.

With every step, the night reveals,
Visions cloaked in tender light.
In the haze, the spirit heals,
As wandering souls take flight.

Through the fog, the past awakes,
Memories dance in soft embrace.
Awakening from sleep's mistakes,
Into the dreamer's sacred space.

Dance of Shadows in Midnight's Grasp

In the grasp of midnight's hand,
Shadows twirl, a haunting light.
Stories told in silent band,
Veils of darkness twinkling bright.

Figures play in flick'ring glow,
Each movement a secret shared.
In this dance, the heart must flow,
With the whispers, unprepared.

Ghostly echoes fill the air,
Breathless sighs of those long gone.
In the dark, we find our pair,
In the dance until the dawn.

Every step, a tale unfolds,
Of love lost and paths untraced.
In shadows' waltz, the spirit holds,
The dreams that time has interlaced.

As night gives way to fading stars,
The dance fades into morning's light.
Yet forever, within our scars,
The shadows dance, both day and night.

Secrets of the Silver-Laced Fen

In the quiet of the night,
Silver threads weave through the air,
Whispers dance upon the breeze,
Secrets linger everywhere.

Moonlight drapes the ancient trees,
Casting shadows on the ground,
Each step echoes tales of old,
In this sacred place, profound.

Rippling waters softly sigh,
Reflecting dreams of lost despair,
Hidden truths beneath the reeds,
Where silence reigns, and none dare.

With the dawn, the secrets fade,
Beneath the waking sun's embrace,
Yet in hearts, those whispers dwell,
Carried forth, a gentle trace.

Shadows Unraveled at Dusk

As the sun dips low to rest,
Shadows lengthen, twisting wide,
Colors merge in softest hues,
Night reveals what day must hide.

Beneath the boughs, a rustling sound,
Creatures stir and come alive,
With each breath, a story spun,
Where illusions start to thrive.

Ghostly forms drift through the air,
Carried on the gentle wind,
In the twilight's dusky veil,
Lost and found, where paths have been.

Fingers of dusk gently grasp,
The heartbeats wrapped in fading light,
In the wane of day's embrace,
Eyes unveil the hidden sight.

Phantoms of the Lonely Marsh

In the marsh where willows weep,
Phantoms wander, soft and slow,
Secrets whispered on the breeze,
To the moon that casts its glow.

Fog enfolds the quiet paths,
Veiling steps with mystery,
Each footfall stirs the stillness,
Echoes lost in history.

Laughter haunts the brittle reeds,
Shadows flicker, pale and thin,
Nature cradles cherished dreams,
For all who dare to enter in.

Beyond the fog, a world awaits,
Bound in silence, time stands still,
With every breath, a tale unfolds,
Of forgotten hopes and will.

Lurking Softly in Midnight's Fold

In the depths where shadows creep,
Lurking softly 'neath the stars,
Silent watchers, hidden eyes,
Listen closely to our scars.

Midnight holds a tender grace,
Cradling fears within her fold,
In the dark, the heart reveals,
Stories waiting to be told.

With each whisper on the night,
Ancient echoes find their place,
Upon the lips of sleeping dreams,
Unfurling slowly, soft embrace.

Yet as dawn begins to break,
The secrets fade with morning light,
But in the folds of midnight's cloak,
Lies the depth of endless night.

Whispers in the Mist

In the stillness of the dawn,
Soft whispers drift and yawn.
Secrets held within the haze,
Nature's voice in gentle ways.

Echoes dance with evening light,
Misty tendrils take their flight.
Gone are shadows of the night,
While daybreak paints the world bright.

Footsteps whisper on the ground,
Fleeting moments all around.
In the coolness of the air,
Silent stories linger there.

Leaves are rustling, secrets shared,
Softly spoken, none compared.
Misty shrouds in soft embrace,
Breathe in the magic of this place.

As the world begins to wake,
In the mist, our spirits shake.
Embrace the whispers and the peace,
In these moments, find release.

Reflections in the Twilight Marsh

In the twilight's soft embrace,
Marshes hold a gentle grace.
Ripples dance on water's face,
Time slows down at nature's pace.

Cattails whisper tales of old,
In the silence, stories told.
Reflections shimmer, softly gleam,
Caught within a fading dream.

Frogs croak softly, crickets hum,
Nature's chorus, a sweet drum.
As the sun dips low and red,
Shadows stretch, the day has fled.

Moonrise casts a silver glow,
To the marsh, where secrets flow.
Every echo, every call,
In this haven, we feel small.

Capturing the fleeting light,
In the stillness of the night.
Loss and longing intertwine,
In the marsh, our dreams align.

Flickering Shadows Over the Mire

Flickering shadows come alive,
Where the restless echoes thrive.
Over the mire, they take flight,
Hidden wonders, dark and bright.

Moonlit beams through branches weave,
In the stillness, we believe.
Figures dance in mystic glow,
Drawing eyes to what we know.

Mire reflects a ghostly sight,
Shapes of dreams in waning light.
Voices whisper through the trees,
Carried softly on the breeze.

Footprints lost in tangled roots,
Nature's melody, it salutes.
Here in shadows, time stands still,
In the quiet, we find thrill.

As the night begins to fade,
In this magic, unafraid.
Flickering dreams will reappear,
In our hearts, forever near.

Veils of Haze in the Dusk

Veils of haze envelop night,
Gently dimming fading light.
As the stars begin to shine,
Whispers weave through vines entwined.

Colors blend in twilight's sigh,
Muted tones that softly lie.
Pinks and purples softly sway,
Here in dusk we find our way.

Mysterious paths lead us on,
In the quiet, dreams are drawn.
Every step, a fleeting chance,
In this evening's soft romance.

Echoes linger, time grows old,
Stories waiting to be told.
In the dusky veil's embrace,
We discover our own place.

As the night unfolds its arms,
Wrapped in nature's silent charms.
Veils of haze, a gentle guide,
Together, we will abide.

Harmonies of Flickering Lights

Stars weave patterns in the night,
Whispers dance with the moonlight.
Gentle breezes, secrets share,
In this magic, time's laid bare.

Echoes of laughter, soft and clear,
Calling memories, drawing near.
With every flicker, stories bloom,
In this space, we shed our gloom.

Colors mingle, twilight's art,
Painting dreams upon the heart.
Harmony found in shadows long,
In the silence, we belong.

Through the darkness, hope ignites,
In the symphony of lights.
Together as one, we take flight,
In the stillness of the night.

Each spark a promise, bright and true,
In the dance, I find you too.
Flickering tales of love and grace,
In this realm, we find our place.

In the Heart of the Shrouded Fen

Mist rolls softly, veiling sight,
Where shadows linger, draped in night.
Footsteps pause on marshy ground,
Echoes of silence all around.

Moonbeams filter through the trees,
Carrying whispers on the breeze.
Secrets buried in the mud,
Tales of old in soft, thick thud.

Frogs croak out their ancient call,
Nature's chorus, a lovely thrall.
In this wild, forgotten space,
The breath of history leaves its trace.

Ripples break the mirror still,
Where water meets the rolling hill.
And as the night unfurls its cloak,
In every heart, a dream awoke.

In the heart of this hidden land,
Life breathes gently, hand in hand.
Among the reeds, we come to see,
Traces of what used to be.

Wistful Lament by the Waterside

Softly lapping at the shore,
Whispers of ages, tales of yore.
Each wave a sigh, a gentle breath,
In its rhythm, echoes of death.

Beneath the sky's deep, endless blue,
Hearts reveal what's tried and true.
Memories drift on currents deep,
In the waters, secrets keep.

Once laughter rang through sunlit years,
Now only shadows and silent tears.
As the evening sun departs,
The waters cradle broken hearts.

Wistful sighs on the gentle breeze,
Rustling leaves, a soft reprise.
The melody of days gone past,
A lament that forever lasts.

By the waters, dreams unfold,
In the stillness, stories told.
A bittersweet farewell takes flight,
Beneath the stars, into the night.

Twilight's Veil on the Forgotten Marsh

Twilight cloaks the world in gray,
As dusk unfolds the end of day.
Within the reeds, a soft refrain,
Where nature's heart knows joy and pain.

Shadows stretch, a quiet grace,
Glancing through this hidden place.
Every rustle tells a tale,
Of whispered dreams that will not fail.

The sky ignites with hues of flame,
While crickets call, none feel the same.
In this expanse, a story brews,
Bathed in twilight's gentle hues.

As starlight peeks through branches wide,
The marsh holds secrets deep inside.
A sanctuary for lost souls,
Where twilight's magic gently rolls.

Beneath the veil, the past holds tight,
In whispers shared beneath the night.
A tapestry in softest strands,
The forgotten marsh, in stillness stands.

Soft Glow of Twilight Whispers

The sun dips low, the sky ablaze,
With hues of pink and soft displays.
The day whispers secrets, soft and low,
In gentle breezes, dreams will flow.

Stars awaken, twinkling shy,
As night descends, the world will sigh.
Moonlight dances on the lake,
A tranquil scene, as hearts awake.

Crickets chirp a lullaby sweet,
While shadows lengthen, softly meet.
The air, a canvas painted bright,
With twilight's glow, a cherished sight.

With every breath, the night draws near,
Each whispered word, we hold so dear.
In this twilight, we find our peace,
A moment held, where worries cease.

Beneath the sky, our spirits soar,
Finding solace on the shore.
With twilight's whispers, love unfolds,
A story told, as night beholds.

Constellations Dimming in the Fog

Through swirling mist, the stars retreat,
In shadows thick, they lose their beat.
Whispers of night, a veiled embrace,
As constellations drift from place.

The moon, a ghost, concealed and shy,
Guides us softly as we sigh.
Fog hugs the earth, a dampened sound,
Where secrets lost may yet be found.

Each step we take in muted grace,
Finding solace in this space.
The world, a blur, yet dreams align,
In fog's embrace, the heart can shine.

All the while, memories fade,
As the night serenades unmade.
We grasp at stars and hope to cling,
To the faded songs the silence brings.

Yet in this shroud, we learn to see,
The hidden truths of you and me.
As constellations dim and slip,
Our souls embark on a silent trip.

Luminous Secrets of the Ether

In the vast expanse, whispers rise,
Through cosmic winds and ancient skies.
Bursts of light, a distant dance,
In ethereal realms, we dare to prance.

Unraveled tales, the stars impart,
Each twinkle holds a beating heart.
With every glow, we seek to learn,
The secrets hidden, our hopes discern.

Nebulas bloom in vibrant waves,
Carrying dreams of those who brave.
And through the void, a song is sung,
Of galaxies new and old, forever young.

In moments still, we rise and float,
On beams of light, like a tiny boat.
With every breath, we feel the fate,
Of luminous dreams we navigate.

Through endless worlds, our spirits roam,
In shared wonders, we find our home.
The luminous secrets of the night,
Awake our souls to the endless light.

Veil of Muffled Silhouettes

Beneath the cloak of evening's sigh,
Shadows dance, as time slips by.
A stillness creeps, the world drapes low,
In a shroud of dusk, where dreams may grow.

Figures blur in muted shades,
Where whispers linger, softly fade.
Footsteps hush on cobblestone,
In twilight's fold, we feel alone.

Yet in the gloom, connections spark,
Hidden stories within the dark.
Each silhouette, a tale to tell,
Of life's embrace, its gentle swell.

The night unfurls with stars above,
Each twinkling light a whispered love.
A veil adorned with memories held,
In muffled tones, their magic swelled.

As dusk enfolds, we hold our breath,
In this liminal space, we dance with death.
Veil of silhouettes, soft and clear,
With every heartbeat, we draw near.

Resonance of the Dimming Light

Whispers fade as day withdraws,
The sun sets low with gentle pause.
Shadows stretch upon the ground,
In silence, echoes softly sound.

With each glow that starts to wane,
The night reveals its tender gain.
Stars awake with watches bright,
Guardians of the deepening night.

Voices carried on the breeze,
Tales of love and memories.
In twilight's arms, we dare to dream,
In shadows cast, our wishes gleam.

The fireflies dance, a fleeting spark,
As darkness reigns and light embarks.
In symmetry, the world aligns,
A harmony in fleeting signs.

So let us breathe the dimming light,
Where hopes converge and dreams take flight.
In the hush, we find our way,
Resonance calls at close of day.

Chasing Phantoms in the Fens

In the mist where willows sway,
Shadows linger, lost in play.
Whispers haunt the quiet night,
Chasing phantoms out of sight.

Footsteps echo, soft and slow,
Through the marsh where secrets grow.
Flickers dance like fleeting dreams,
Caught in twilight's gentle beams.

Moonlight spills on waters deep,
Where lost loves and memories sleep.
A silent song begins to weave,
As fog unveils what we believe.

Figures drift among the reeds,
Stories born from yearning needs.
In this realm of soft and soft,
We chase what lingers, yet is lost.

So wander here, and let time bend,
In the fens where echoes blend.
With open hearts, we'll find our way,
Chasing phantoms, come what may.

Murmurs of the Misty Vale

In the vale where shadows lie,
Murmurs rise like whispers shy.
Fog cascades through ancient trees,
Carrying tales upon the breeze.

Footfalls hush on emerald ground,
Nature's symphony surrounds.
Softly breathing, life awakes,
Every sigh, a promise makes.

Dewdrops glisten on the grass,
Moments fleeting, yet they pass.
In the mist, we find our peace,
For the heart beats, fears release.

Spirit dancers drift and sway,
Painting dreams in shades of gray.
With each murmur, we align,
Threads of fate and love entwine.

So linger here, embrace the chill,
In the vale where time stands still.
Murmurs guide us through the night,
In the mist, we find our light.

A Dance of Light Beneath the Haze

Beneath the haze, the world awakes,
In gentle moves, the silence quakes.
Light interweaves with shadow's art,
A dance unfolds, a tender heart.

Colors blend in scalar grace,
As daybreak kisses every space.
Each brush of light, a painter's touch,
Transforming all, it means so much.

In twirls of gold and silken rays,
We lose ourselves in nature's plays.
The air is thick with magic's breath,
As life ignites, defying death.

Step by step, the rhythm flows,
Join the dance where beauty grows.
Underneath the softest glow,
We find the essence we all know.

So join the sway, release your fears,
In this moment, wipe your tears.
For in the haze, our spirits rise,
A dance of light beneath the skies.

Wings of the Night's Embrace

In whispers the moon casts its glow,
Shadows dance where soft breezes flow.
The stars, like jewels, twinkle bright,
Holding secrets of the night.

Trees sway gently in the dark,
Awakening dreams with a spark.
Comfort resides in the still air,
As night wraps us in tender care.

A lullaby plays through the leaves,
As the world rests and softly breathes.
Crickets sing, their songs entwine,
In harmony with the divine.

Wings unfurl in a silent flight,
Carrying hopes into the night.
With every heartbeat, dreams take wing,
In the magic that twilight can bring.

Embrace the calm, the quiet near,
Trust in the night, release all fear.
For in this space, our spirits soar,
Wings of the night, forevermore.

Faint Echo of a Forgotten Song

In the hush of the breaking dawn,
Echoes linger of what's long gone.
A melody lost in the breeze,
Whispers of time beneath the trees.

Ancient rhythms softly play,
Carried on winds that drift away.
Notes entwined with the morning dew,
Fleeting moments, yet so true.

Through forgotten paths, it weaves,
A song remembered in the leaves.
Haunting strains of a distant past,
Calling us home, both deep and vast.

Each chord resonates with lost dreams,
Faint as the sunlight's gentle beams.
In shadows where memories blend,
A song persists, it will not end.

Faint echo, sweet and profound,
In nature's heart, it can be found.
For every soul that longs to sing,
A forgotten song it will bring.

Enigma Wrapped in Soft Shadows

In twilight's hush, a mystery brews,
Crafted in shades of soft, muted hues.
Veils of fog cloak the unseen,
Whispers linger where shadows glean.

Figures fade into the night,
An enigma wrapped, a fleeting sight.
Secrets hidden in the dark,
As silence draws a gentle arc.

Eyes that glimmer with untold tales,
Float like ships on misty gales.
Every heartbeat, a clue to find,
In the folds of the night, entwined.

A dance of whispers flits and sways,
In the soft shadows, time decays.
Yet hope lingers, a flickering flame,
In shadows, we discover our name.

Wrapped in layers of dusk's embrace,
We seek to uncover a hidden place.
An enigma awaits in the night,
In soft shadows, we find our light.

Resonance of Twilight Spirits

In the quiet of the failing light,
Spirits stir with the coming night.
Footsteps echo on the path,
Drawing near in their gentle swath.

The air is thick with tales untold,
Whispers of wisdom, both brave and bold.
Fragrant blooms in twilight's glow,
Awake as the night begins to flow.

In the dance of dusk and dawn,
Life's rhythms swell, never withdrawn.
Breathe in deep, the night's embrace,
As spirits gather in this space.

Each flicker of fireflies' flight,
Guides us through the fading light.
Resonance of hearts and souls,
In twilight's warmth, the darkness rolls.

As the stars twinkle and twine,
In unity, we intertwine.
With every breath, spirits align,
In the resonance, we find the divine.

Dance of Ember and Vapor

Flickering flames in the dark,
Whispers of warmth, a spark.
Twisting shadows, bright and free,
A ballet of light, a fiery sea.

Against the night, they swirl and glide,
Embraced by the air, they won't hide.
Cinder and smoke, a fragile trace,
In the stillness, a mesmerizing chase.

Amidst the dusk, they pirouette,
Lost in the rhythm, a sweet duet.
Each breath of fire wears a veil,
As ember's dance begins to pale.

Time drifts by, the embers fade,
A memory of light, serenely made.
Yet in the silence, they remain,
A dance of vapor, a haunting refrain.

In the shadows where dreams reside,
Embers and vapors unite, collide.
They twine their fate in the night,
A radiant glow, a fleeting sight.

Charcoal Whispers under the Moonlight

In the quiet glow, the charcoal speaks,
Stories of nights, of shadows and peaks.
Lines on the canvas, secrets unfold,
Figures emerge, from echoes of old.

Under the moon's soft silver light,
Artistry awakens in gentle flight.
Embraced by the calm, the whispers flow,
As charcoal dances with the night's glow.

Each stroke a tale, untold, unseen,
Delicate dreams in shades between.
The heart of the artist, bare and true,
In charcoal's embrace, a world anew.

Night stretches wide, an endless page,
As stories weave through the artist's sage.
A gallery born from breath and sigh,
In the charcoal play, we laugh and cry.

With every shadow that graces the scene,
Moonlit whispers, soft and serene.
Charcoal holds what visions yearn,
In the depths of night, we always return.

Reflections of Twilight's Breeze

As twilight descends, the world must pause,
Beneath a sky that softly draws.
A breeze dances through the gentle leaves,
Whispers of twilight, a heart that believes.

Colors blend in a warm embrace,
Nature's palette, a tranquil space.
Rippling waters catch the glow,
Mirrored moments, a soft-flowing show.

In the hush where day meets night,
Shadows stir in fading light.
An echo lingers, secrets shared,
In twilight's grasp, we are ensnared.

As dreams unfold in fading sun,
The breeze hums softly, day is done.
Reflections shimmer, softly tease,
In the twilight's arms, we find our ease.

Each sigh of wind, a gentle song,
In twilight's dance, we all belong.
Harmony found in evening's grace,
As shadows blend, we find our place.

Mist-Wreathed Dreams of the Fen

In the fen where silence reigns,
Misty whispers, embrace the plains.
Dreams are woven in the dew,
A tapestry crafted, soft and true.

Ghostly figures glide through night,
Crickets sing, the stars ignite.
Nature's breath, a soft refrain,
In this world, we lose the pain.

Shadows merge with the morning light,
Tales of wonder, a tranquil sight.
Every droplet tells a story,
In fen's embrace, we find our glory.

Dreams take flight on the misty breeze,
Floating freely through the trees.
The heart pulsates with instinct's drum,
In these fleeting moments, we can succumb.

Awakening thoughts amidst the flow,
In the fen, where time moves slow.
Mist-wreathed dreams breathe life anew,
In the veil of dawn, all feels so true.

The Allure of Misty Horizons

Misty shades embrace the dawn,
Whispers dance on gentle winds,
Mountains loom, a ghostly throng,
In silence, nature rescinds.

Waves of fog like curtains fall,
Colors blend, a soft embrace,
Every glance, a silent call,
Lost in time, we find our place.

Birds aloft on fragile veils,
Songs unspoken fill the air,
As if dreaming through the trails,
Where the sky and earth lay bare.

Rivers swirl with morning light,
Secrets murmured, none behold,
Interwoven, day and night,
Boundless stories yet untold.

In this realm of twilight dreams,
Where our thoughts and wishes flow,
Misty horizons draw us near,
To the beauty of the unknown.

Shadows and Reflections at Dusk's Veil

Beneath the arch of twilight's grace,
Shadows stretch to kiss the ground,
The sun retreats, a warm embrace,
Echoes whisper all around.

Reflections glimmer on the stream,
Flickering lights like distant stars,
In this soft, enchanting dream,
We trace paths beyond the scars.

Crickets sing a lullaby,
Their chorus builds, a sweet refrain,
As day fades into twilight's sigh,
Hope and longing intertwine.

Branches sway in gentle breeze,
Carrying tales from days of old,
In dusk's arms, we find our ease,
Life's mysteries silently unfold.

Underneath the starry veil,
We gather moments, pure and bright,
In shadows deep, we feel the trail,
Of dreams igniting in the night.

Embered Spirits Over Marshy Waters

Amid the reeds, the shadows play,
Embers dance on the mirrored pond,
A flicker's grace, a soft ballet,
Where spirits tread and love responds.

Moonlight spills like silver beams,
Painting paths on marshy floors,
Every ripple tells of dreams,
Whispers echo through the shores.

Fires burn in hearts so bright,
Reflections of the night's delight,
In the stillness, secrets hover,
As the water holds our wonder.

A chorus of the night insects,
Their serenade, a haunting sound,
While in the mist, the past connects,
Eternal moments, lost but found.

Through the fog, we find our way,
Tracing paths of light and shade,
Embered spirits come to play,
In the dance where memories wade.

The Alchemy of Fog and Flicker

In the cradle of fog's embrace,
Where shadows blend and shapes transform,
Mysteries hide in every space,
While flickers of light begin to swarm.

The world dissolves in silver hues,
Softened edges, a tranquil scene,
As nature's palette gently imbues,
Life's fleeting whispers in between.

With each step, the night unfolds,
Stories woven in the air,
In flickering lights, magic holds,
The heart's desire laid bare.

Time stands still on pathways lost,
In the alchemy of now and then,
Every breath an ancient cost,
Where we find ourselves again.

In this realm, our spirits soar,
With fog and flicker, we align,
Through the veils, we yearn for more,
In this dance, we intertwine.

Murmurs of the Ethereal

In the hush of twilight's breath,
Whispers dance through silken air.
Stars awaken from their sleep,
Casting dreams without a care.

Moonlight drapes the world in silk,
A gentle touch upon the ground.
Echoes linger, softly felt,
Bathed in night's elusive sound.

Shadows weave a tapestry,
Among the trees, a secret thread.
Every sigh a story told,
As ancient echoes softly spread.

The night unfolds its velvet cloak,
Crickets sing their serenade.
In the realm where spirits glide,
Magic comes, no need for jade.

Fleeting moments, shaped like dreams,
Caught between the worlds we know.
Murmurs rise and softly fall,
In the stillness, hearts aglow.

Faint Gleams in the Gloaming

As dusk descends, the colors blend,
With hints of gold and softest gray.
Faint gleams spark in the fading light,
Painting the world in a playful way.

The skyline blushes, bows in grace,
Clouds become a canvas bright.
Nature's brush, with tender strokes,
Crafts a scene of pure delight.

Birdsong lingers on the wind,
A gentle hymn at day's retreat.
In these moments, time stands still,
Magic fills the air, discreet.

The sun dips low, a final bow,
While shadows stretch and softly creep.
A serene hush blankets the earth,
Inviting dreams in twilight's sweep.

Within the gloaming, secrets hide,
In fading light where wishes lay.
Faint gleams shimmer, guiding hope,
Through the night and into day.

Ephemeral Flames of Dusk

Fires flicker in the evening breeze,
Ephemeral and bright, they sway.
Each flame whispers a story lost,
In the shadows where flickers play.

Crimson hues bleed into the night,
As day gives way to twilight's call.
A dance of embers, wild and free,
In a hush that urges us to sprawl.

Glimmers fade beyond the trees,
As stars awaken, bold and clear.
In the stillness, warmth remains,
An echo of the sun's bright cheer.

Moments flicker, easily missed,
Like fireflies in a dusky throng.
Ephemeral flames, brief yet bright,
Remind us where we all belong.

In this twilight, grasp the light,
Cherish each flicker, hold it tight.
For dusk will weave its final tale,
As night uncovers quiet fright.

Resonance of the Silent Woods

In the woods where silence reigns,
Nature's heart beats soft and low.
Echoes linger in the shade,
Carried by the whispering flow.

Leaves murmur secrets to the trees,
A language only they can share.
Every rustle, every sigh,
Is a song played in tranquil air.

Morning light spills through the boughs,
Dancing on the forest floor.
Sunbeams weave through tranquil greens,
Inviting life to softly soar.

With each step, a story wakes,
In patches where the wildflowers bloom.
The scent of earth and pine entwined,
Fills the woods with nature's perfume.

In the stillness, find your peace,
Let the resonance guide you near.
Where the silent woods embrace the heart,
And whispers calm each hidden fear.

Shimmers of the Fading Light

In the twilight's gentle grace,
Soft shadows start to dance,
Whispers speak of time's embrace,
As day gives dark a chance.

Stars awaken, shy and bright,
Casting dreams across the ground,
While the world holds its breath tight,
In silence, hope is found.

Golden hues begin to fade,
Blushing skies unveil their tears,
Every promise softly laid,
Beneath the weight of years.

Time meanders, slow and sweet,
Gathering secrets in the night,
Each heartbeat a rhythmic beat,
In the shimmers of fading light.

As the dark embraces all,
Stars intertwine as they gleam,
In this quiet, enchanted hall,
Dreams awaken, softly beam.

Lost Tales from the Misty Realm

Veils of fog enshroud the glade,
Hidden paths of whispered lore,
Echoes in the silence played,
Each step leads to tales of yore.

Phantoms of the forest glide,
Their stories linger in the air,
Wrapped in twilight, spirits bide,
Every breath a whispered prayer.

Shadows dance on ancient stones,
Nature weaves her mystic thread,
Secrets whispered, lost in tones,
Of lives lived and long since dead.

In the mist, forgotten sighs,
Haunt the branches, sway the trees,
Every flutter, every rise,
Carries stories on the breeze.

Through the haze, a truth stands tall,
Where time and space entwine and blend,
In the heart of the misty thrall,
Lost tales patiently ascend.

Echoes Hovering in the Burnished Air

In the warmth of sunlit glow,
Echoes pulse in flowing streams,
Carrying whispers soft and slow,
Alive within our waking dreams.

Each moment drips with golden hues,
The world alive with vibrant sounds,
Harmony in every muse,
In resonance, our heart abounds.

Waves of laughter paint the skies,
As time flows like the river's face,
In glimmers found, truth never lies,
Every heartbeat finds its place.

Stillness speaks in shimmers bright,
Filling voids with gentle grace,
Echoes hover, pure delight,
In our souls, they find their space.

To the rhythm of our sighs,
We dance beneath the burnished air,
In every twirl, the spirit flies,
Echoes linger, free as air.

Flickers of the Fen's Hidden Lore

In the still of the fen's embrace,
Flickers spark between the reeds,
Secrets whisper in the chase,
Of every story that proceeds.

Moonlight shatters on the sway,
Casting shadows, weaving tales,
Through the night and into day,
Where the longing heart prevails.

Creatures stir in cloaked disguise,
Breath of the night, a mystic lore,
With every flicker, a surprise,
In the depths, the spirits soar.

Ancient wisdom fills the air,
Softly weaving in and out,
In the fen, a sacred lair,
Where no doubt can bloom or sprout.

With each whisper of the breeze,
Stories dance along the shore,
Hidden truths among the trees,
Flickers show the fen's lost lore.

The Fog's Embrace at Evening's Edge

The fog creeps in, a gentle shroud,
Whispering secrets beneath the cloud.
Soft shadows dance on twilight's seam,
Veiling the world in a silken dream.

The trees stand tall, their forms unclear,
Muffled whispers that only I hear.
Stars dimly flicker, lost in the gray,
The night enfolds as twilight fades away.

A beacon glows from the lighthouse high,
Guiding the boats through the misty sigh.
Each breath a wonder, each moment still,
Wrapped in silence, the night's sweet thrill.

Shadows entwine in the dusk's soft glow,
Footsteps fade where the wild winds blow.
The fog's embrace, a tender caress,
Cradling dreams in a world of less.

Time slips softly through the fog's tight hold,
A tapestry woven with threads of gold.
In evening's grasp, the heart takes flight,
Lost in the magic of the incoming night.

Luminous Refrains from the Mire's Breath

In the mire where shadows weave,
Luminous refrains begin to cleave.
Dancing lights on a surface grim,
Waltzing softly on Nature's whim.

Mist rises slow from the ground below,
Softly bright, like a whispered glow.
Echoed laughter from depths so dark,
Songs of the night, igniting a spark.

Reflections drift in a ghostly haze,
Beckoning thoughts through a murky maze.
A chorus echoes with every breath,
Inviting all to forget the death.

Footsteps find rhythm on squelching ground,
In the loom of the unseen sound.
With each refrain, the heart feels alive,
In this mire where the lost thrive.

So let the light guide from afar,
Through the bogs to a brighter star.
The mire hums a melody sweet,
In the night where reflections meet.

Echoes Through the Ethereal Mist

In twilight's grasp, the echoes play,
Through the mist, they weave and sway.
Voices whisper from realms unknown,
Carried softly like seeds that've blown.

The ether drips with layers of sound,
Notes of longing wrap all around.
Each echo a tale, a distant call,
Resounding gently till shadows fall.

Pale figures drift in the silent breath,
Silent stories of life and death.
Awash in whispers, the night takes form,
Guiding the way through the gathering storm.

The mist embraces like a lover's grace,
Years of sorrow, a tender space.
Each note a memory, each sigh a dream,
Floating softly on the moonlit stream.

Through this haze, the heart will roam,
Seeking solace, a place called home.
In echoes found, we lose and find,
The ethereal mist, a soft unwind.

Glimmers of Ghosts on Still Waters

On still waters, ghosts begin to glide,
Glimmers of light where the memories hide.
Flickers of past touch the surface clear,
Whispers of love that linger near.

Reflections tremble as ripples break,
Hints of the stories that time would unmake.
In the quiet night, the spirits wane,
Seeping softly like whispered rain.

As the moon casts silver upon the lake,
Echoes arise, the silence they break.
Each glimmer a heartbeat from long ago,
Carrying tales of joy and woe.

The water shimmers beneath the stars,
A canvas painted with ancient scars.
Glimmers of ghosts that shimmer and sway,
Forever entwined in an endless play.

The night holds secrets that spirits share,
In the stillness, there's magic in the air.
With each soft glow on the water's face,
Life dances softly in a haunting embrace.

Glimmers Beneath the Veil

In the hush of night's embrace,
Soft whispers flit and trace.
Glimmers dance on water's face,
Tales of dreams in shadowed space.

Stars awaken one by one,
Beneath the watchful, silver moon.
The world breathes deep, begun anew,
In quietude, life finds its tune.

A path adorned with linden trees,
Traces steps of ancient lore.
Mysteries greet the wandering breeze,
As echoes linger evermore.

In glades where time stands still,
Fleeting moments, bittersweet.
Nature's heart, a gentle thrill,
Plays a symphony soft and fleet.

Awake, oh heart, to night's surreal,
Where fantasies and truths entwine.
Amidst the dusk, there's much to feel,
As glimmers merge, both yours and mine.

Enigmatic Twilight Rhapsody

Twilight drapes the world in shades,
Mysteries in soft cascade.
Colors blend, a silent trade,
Whispers of the night conveyed.

Beneath the trees, shadows play,
Secrets woven, fine and grey.
Each fleeting moment finds its way,
In dusk's embrace, dreams sway.

The horizon speaks in hues,
Blues and purples, nature's muse.
As day retreats, the night renews,
In muted tones, the heart imbues.

Silhouettes of ancient spires,
Reach toward the starry heights.
The twilight air, a song inspires,
As the world dims, joy ignites.

In this realm where secrets stir,
The magic lingers, vibrant, pure.
Enigmatic night, as thoughts confer,
In twilight's arms, forever sure.

Ethereal Depths of the Backwater

In stillness rests the hidden deep,
Backwater dreams in silence seep.
Reflections swirl, a lore to keep,
Where ancient whispers softly creep.

Fragrant blooms, in twilight's glow,
Rustle in the gentle flow.
Secrets kept where shadows grow,
Ethereal depths, a magic show.

Amidst the reeds, the coolness thrives,
Crickets sing and water dives.
In harmony, the wild survives,
A tranquil pulse that ever strives.

Here, time's grip begins to fade,
The world beyond seems far away.
Lives entwined, the dance portrayed,
In ethereal depths, we sway.

As twilight beckons, moments blend,
Life's fleeting pulse, a sacred trend.
Beneath the surface, hearts transcend,
In backwater dreams, we find our friend.

Faint Flickers Beneath the Clouded Sky

Beneath the clouds, dim lights appear,
Faint flickers whisper, drawing near.
A gentle pulse, a heartbeat clear,
Stardust magic fills the sphere.

Hazy dreams on velvet ground,
Softly woven, lost then found.
In every heartbeat, love's profound,
A melody, a tender sound.

The skyline kissed by muted hues,
Hints of silver, deeper blues.
Each flicker speaks of hope anew,
In twilight's grasp, the world imbues.

Veils of mist, a world concealed,
Yet through the haze, hearts revealed.
In quiet moments, fate unsealed,
A bond where dreams are gently healed.

Faint flickers ride the night's embrace,
Finding solace in their space.
Beneath the clouds, a sacred place,
Where every heartbeat leaves a trace.

Glistening Echoes of Dim Memories

In shadows where the silence dwells,
A dance of light, a tale it tells.
Faded whispers, a soft embrace,
Glistening echoes, a lost place.

Time weaves threads of silver and gold,
Stories linger, long untold.
Each heartbeat, a haunting refrain,
Carried softly through the rain.

Memories shimmer, like stars that glide,
In the depths where dreamers reside.
The past a canvas, colors set free,
A tapestry spun, eternally.

Yet in the stillness, shadows play,
Drawing forth night from the day.
As visions fade with the setting sun,
A glistening echo, forever spun.

Veiled Lanterns by the Water's Edge

Softly glowing, lanterns weep,
Secrets held in waters deep.
The night whispers tales of old,
Veiled in silver and pure gold.

Ripples dance with a gentle sigh,
Carrying dreams that quickly fly.
Each flicker, a spark of delight,
Guiding lost souls through the night.

Reflections shimmer, soft and warm,
Amidst the shadows, a calming charm.
Beneath the surface, whispers blend,
As time weaves on, no bitter end.

The calming lull of the gentle tide,
Where secrets and mysteries reside.
In the stillness, hearts align,
Veiled lanterns shine, forever divine.

Whispers of the Moonlit Marsh

In the hush of the marshy glade,
Moonlight kisses, shadows cascade.
Each whisper calls from the depths below,
Where secrets dance in a silvery glow.

Frogs croak softly, a rhythmic tone,
Echoing softly, yet not alone.
Crickets chirp in the warm night air,
In this hush, enchantments flare.

The silver pool reflects the sky,
As dreams and visions slip on by.
From twilight's grasp, the night is born,
Woven in magic, softly worn.

Together we dwell, much like the rest,
In the cradle of nature, we're blessed.
As time flows on like the silent stream,
The whispers linger, woven in dream.

Lament of the Haze-Kissed Night

Beneath a blanket of misty grey,
The night softly whispers, holding sway.
In every corner, shadows creep,
The sorrowed heart, forever deep.

Haze-kissed dreams float softly by,
A melancholic, tender sigh.
Every breath carries the weight of time,
Each heartbeat lost in unsung rhyme.

Stars flicker faintly in endless dark,
Fading hopes leave but a mark.
Wrapped in silence, pain takes flight,
In a lament of the fading light.

Yet in the stillness, beauty hides,
Though grief lingers, hope abides.
For in the depths of night's woven plight,
Lies the promise of a new day's light.

Glistening Traces of the Past

Memories whisper through the trees,
A touch of gold in fading light.
Footsteps echo on the ground,
Carrying tales of lost delight.

Fragments glimmer in the brook,
As time's currents softly flow.
Each ripple sings a secret song,
Of moments cherished long ago.

In shadows cast by evening's grace,
Stories linger in the air.
Glistening traces of the past,
A legacy beyond compare.

Old photographs in twilight's glow,
Hold echoes of familiar smiles.
Through them, we wander back in time,
Traveling countless, winding miles.

So pause and breathe the fragrant air,
Let history unveil its art.
In every trace and every line,
We find a piece of our own heart.

The Veil Between Worlds

Where shadows dance with flickering light,
A curtain sways in the night air.
Whispers of dreams float on the breeze,
Hidden realms beyond compare.

A doorway whispers in the still,
Illumined by the moon's soft glow.
Pass through the veil, hear the call,
Of secrets only night can show.

In stillness lies a magic rare,
Threads weave between the seen and unseen.
Reality bends, time collapses,
As we drift into realms pristine.

Echoes of voices, faint but clear,
Tangle like ivy in the trees.
With every footfall, believe the truth,
Awakened by the night's deep pleas.

So walk with courage through the veil,
For every step brings light anew.
In that space between what is,
A world unfolds, just for you.

Gaze into the Embrace of the Unknown

Beneath the stars, a journey calls,
Whispers linger on the breeze.
Open your heart, let worries go,
In the vastness, find your ease.

The night sky beckons, dark and deep,
With mysteries shining bright above.
Dare to look beyond the veil,
For in the unknown, there's love.

Each twinkling light, a story shared,
Of dreams that soared and hopes that fell.
Gaze into the cosmic sea,
Where every star holds a secret spell.

Let curiosity guide your path,
With wonder as your guiding star.
Embrace the void, the endless quest,
Adventure awaits, no matter how far.

With courage wrapped in starlight's shroud,
Step boldly into the vast unknown.
For in its depths, you'll find your truth,
A journey carved in the heart of stone.

Dappled Shadows on an Evening Canvas

In twilight's brush, the world awakes,
Colors blend with whispers low.
Dappled shadows play on ground,
Painting tales of ebb and flow.

Golden rays through branches peek,
Kissing petals with warm grace.
Each hue a brushstroke, soft and fine,
Entwining nature's sweet embrace.

Rustling leaves in playful dance,
Echo laughter from the trees.
As daylight yields to night's romance,
The canvas holds our memories.

In the hush of earth's soft sigh,
Find the peace that evening brings.
Dappled shadows whisper secrets,
In rhythm with the heart that sings.

So linger here, in this sweet hour,
Let colors flood your very soul.
For life, like art, is meant to flow,
With dappled shadows, we feel whole.

Glowing Reflections in the Haunting Haze

In twilight's embrace, whispers arise,
Soft glimmers dance, beneath the skies.
Shadows are weaving, dreams take flight,
The world turns golden, surrendering light.

A mirror of silence, the lake it spreads,
Each ripple a story, where magic treads.
Phantoms of dusk, in shimmering grace,
Gently they linger, time can't erase.

Through mist-laden paths, the echoes flow,
Enigmas awaken, tales in tow.
Brightened reflections, secrets unveil,
Embers of memory, a ghostly trail.

The haunting haze keeps shadows near,
Yet hope ignites, casting off fear.
In glowing embrace, the night shall sway,
As stars knit the dreams that guide our way.

A Tapestry of Light and Mist

Threads of twilight, woven in air,
A canvas of colors, beyond compare.
Glistening raindrops, they shimmer and fall,
Nature's own artwork, a grand free-for-all.

In the softest sigh, the morning breaks,
Meadows awaken, as sunlight wakes.
With each gentle breeze, the whispers grow,
A tapestry rich, in ebb and flow.

Clouds like dancers, drift through the blue,
Painting horizons, ever anew.
Fleeting moments, caught in the glow,
Breathless together, we savor the show.

Luminous dreams weave through the mist,
In this sacred realm, nothing's amiss.
A melody soft, in nature's embrace,
Unraveled, our worries, we lovingly trace.

Secrets of the Gloaming Fen

Beneath the willow, shadows creep,
An ancient secret, the fen must keep.
Bubbles of twilight, rise and burst,
Among the whispers, the wild things thirst.

Fairy lights twinkle, through leaf and fern,
Illuminating paths, for bold hearts to learn.
Echoes of laughter, in reeds they play,
Magic woven, at close of day.

A hush in the air, as night draws near,
The fen holds its breath, listening clear.
With secrets to share, in whispers they dwell,
Inviting the brave, to dare and to tell.

In moon's tender glow, the waters gleam,
Reflecting the hues of a fading dream.
A world enchanted, where shadows thrive,
Here in the gloaming, the wild comes alive.

Reverberations in the Dusk

The world is hushed, as night descends,
A symphony stirs, where daylight ends.
Notes of the dark, begin their flight,
Whispers of wonder, enshroud the night.

Cicadas sing, in rhythmic delight,
Ballet of shadows, takes to the light.
Stars become lanterns, guiding the way,
Reverberations, of dreams at play.

Silhouettes dance, in the deepening gloom,
Lingering echoes, sweet flowers bloom.
The pulse of existence, soft and entwined,
Embracing the beauty, that lingers behind.

In the canvas of dusk, a portrait appears,
Blending the laughter, with unspoken fears.
Reverberations, where hearts align,
In the gentle embrace of the night we dine.

Vesper's Cloak on the Marsh

Vesper's cloak drapes the night,
Whispers of dusk take flight.
Beneath the waning sky,
Silent shadows drift by.

Purple haze cloaks the reeds,
Where the soft water feeds.
Breezes carry lost dreams,
Fleeting as moonbeams.

Marshland sighs in repose,
Nature's quiet, it knows.
Stars blink, a twinkling call,
Casting light o'er it all.

Echoes dance on the ground,
In this serene surround.
Vesper's song, gentle sway,
Guides the night on its way.

Illuminated Sidelines of the Night

Starlit whispers on the path,
Lighting dreams with gentle wrath.
Each corner holds a story,
In shadows, there's glory.

Streetlamps flicker, soft and low,
Casting warmth against the cold.
In every nook, a heart glows,
Amidst the night, life flows.

Footsteps echo, soft and slow,
On cobblestones kissed by glow.
Illuminated whispers speak,
Of secrets, bold yet meek.

The air is thick with delight,
In the magic of the night.
Stars above, the silent guide,
In their beauty, dreams abide.

Flicker of the Fading Ember

Embers glow as they fade away,
Whispers of warmth in dismay.
Lost in the shadows' embrace,
Time's gentle drift, a slow pace.

Each spark holds a story told,
Of dreams once bright, now dull and cold.
Yet in the dark, hope remains,
Flickers of life in the veins.

Lasting memories ignite,
In the dimming of the light.
Fading fast, yet still they fight,
To clutch onto the night.

With each breath, the ember glows,
In the heart, a warmth bestows.
Bound by what lies deep within,
Whispers of where we have been.

Misted Loneliness in the gloaming

Misted air wraps the silence tight,
A shroud of gray, the fading light.
Loneliness walks beside the trees,
Cradled by soft, whispering breeze.

Gloaming casts a dream-like spell,
In the shadows where echoes dwell.
Heartbeats blend with twilight sighs,
As day and night embrace goodbyes.

Footfalls echo through the haze,
Lost in memory's smoky maze.
A figure wanders, eyes agleam,
Haunted by a fleeting dream.

In the mist, a soft refrain,
Yearning for what's lost to pain.
Loneliness, a fragile thread,
Weaving stories left unsaid.

Secrets Hidden in the Marsh's Veil

In the bog where whispers dwell,
Fog enshrouds the stories swell.
Beneath the leaves, the silence breathes,
Echoes linger, time bequeaths.

Shadows dance with ghostly grace,
Lost in dreams we can't replace.
Veil of green hides truths untold,
In the marsh, secrets unfold.

Ripples stir the water's face,
Footsteps tread a haunting trace.
Each soft sigh, a mystic spell,
Binding all that time won't quell.

Nature's pulse, a rhythmic rhyme,
Tales of love, of loss, of time.
Hidden realms, where visions weave,
In the hush, we dare believe.

With every breath, the marsh exhales,
Filling air with faded tales.
Secrets linger, intertwine,
In the shadows, they align.

Shadows Playing in the Fading Glow

As the sun dips low and dies,
Shadows dance 'neath twilight skies.
Fingers stretch with gentle ease,
Whispers carried by the breeze.

Colors fade to dusky gray,
Chasing light, they slowly sway.
Figures twirl in soft embrace,
Tracing patterns, time's own grace.

The horizon melts to dreams,
Fraying at the darker seams.
Moonlight glimmers, takes its throne,
In the glow, we're not alone.

Voices mix with echoing night,
Lost in moments, pure delight.
Every shadow holds a tale,
In the dusk, we set the sail.

With each flicker, memories swell,
Playing soft, the night's sweet spell.
Until the dawn calls us away,
In shadows, we shall ever stay.

The Lure of Faintly Burning Horizons

Out where the sky meets the sea,
Horizons beckon, wild and free.
Every glow, a siren's song,
Pulls the heart where dreams belong.

Faintly burning, colors blend,
Where every journey finds its end.
A canvas painted with desire,
Setting souls alight with fire.

Waves whisper secrets on the shore,
Promises made, to love once more.
The sun dips low, a fleeting kiss,
In the twilight, find your bliss.

Drifting spirits chase the light,
Filling hearts with pure delight.
Horizons blaze, a vivid dance,
Inviting every soul to chance.

With every dusk, the call is clear,
To follow dreams, to persevere.
The lure of light, a heart's embrace,
In horizons found, we find our place.

Twilight's Lament Over the Quagmire

In the depths where shadows linger,
Twilight weaves its ghostly finger.
A quagmire thick with silent fears,
Echoes soaked in time's own tears.

Softly whispered, tales of woe,
In the dark, lost hopes may glow.
Longing stirs in heavy air,
Twilight's lament, a haunting care.

Beneath the surface, secrets wait,
Pulsing gently, sealing fate.
Memories float like fragile leaves,
Caught in twilight's web, it weaves.

Every sigh, a story spun,
Fading light as day is done.
Through the muck and murky mire,
Heartache lingers, part of the fire.

Yet in this gloom, a spark ignites,
A hope that reaches for the heights.
In the quagmire, we shall find,
Twilight's gift, our hearts aligned.

Dim Beacon in Dusk's Embrace

A glimmer fades in twilight's grasp,
Where shadows dance and moments clasp.
The stars unfold, a timid sight,
As day retreats into the night.

The world exhales, a soft release,
In whispered tones, we find our peace.
The horizon sighs, muted and slow,
As secrets of the darkness grow.

A flicker shines through gentle mist,
Where dreams and dares intertwine, kissed.
The winding paths of night's embrace,
Guide us softly, a tender trace.

Hope lingers still, a fragile thread,
In stories sung of days once fled.
A beacon calls from far and wide,
In dusk's embrace, our fears subside.

We walk the line 'tween light and shade,
In this soft light, our hearts are laid.
The world transforms, a canvas bright,
With every hue of fading light.

Murmurings of the Distant Woodlands

In hidden glades where whispers dwell,
The trees exchange their sacred spells.
A breeze flows through the tangled roots,
While life awakens, softly shoots.

The brook hums low, a lullaby,
As creatures stir, both shy and spry.
In every nook, a tale unfolds,
Of ancient paths and secrets told.

The canopy, a quilt of green,
Hides stories of the unseen.
Each leaf a page, each branch a line,
In nature's tome, forever divine.

The nightingale sings, a haunting tune,
Beneath the watchful gaze of moon.
With every note, the woods awake,
As dreams entwine in twilight's wake.

In every rustle, every sigh,
The woodlands speak, and we comply.
With open hearts, we seek to find,
The murmurs left by nature's mind.

Lingering Hush of the Fading Day

As sunlight bows to night's embrace,
The world falls still, a timeless space.
In hues of red and softest gold,
The evening wraps us, calm and bold.

A distant echo of the sun,
As shadows blend, the day is done.
In twilight's arms, we take our stand,
Where silence speaks, both soft and grand.

The air grows cool, a gentle sigh,
As stars emerge in velvet sky.
The night unfolds with quiet grace,
In every corner, hidden place.

We breathe the dusk, in stillness found,
A lullaby, a soothing sound.
With every heartbeat, time does sway,
In the lingering hush of fading day.

Embrace the night, let worries fade,
In twilight's glow, our dreams are laid.
The world may turn, yet here we stay,
In the lingering hush, we find our way.

As the Voiceless Echoes Drift

In silence bound, the echoes weave,
Where thoughts dissolve and moments cleave.
The shadows cast a gentle glow,
A tapestry of what we know.

Unspoken words in twilight rest,\nWhen hearts unite and
souls invest.
The whispers drift on velvet air,
As time expands beyond compare.

Each breath we take, a fleeting gift,
In stillness where the spirits lift.
Emotions dance in quiet streams,
As dreams unfold in muted beams.

The stars align, their stories flow,
As voiceless echoes softly grow.
In every pause, a world exists,
A realm of thoughts that still persist.

So let us listen to the night,
To voices lost, and hidden light.
In silent echoes, life can spark,
As the voiceless drift through the dark.

Ethereal Lure of the Whispering Waters

Glistening gems beneath the flow,
A tranquil song, soft and low.
Ripples dance in liquid light,
Nature's charm, a pure delight.

Branches sway, a gentle rhyme,
Time stands still, lost in its chime.
Reflections whisper tales untold,
Secrets of the heart unfold.

Misty hues embrace the dawn,
In harmony, the world reborn.
With every current, dreams take flight,
Amidst the glimmering, pure delight.

The laughter of the playful stream,
In every bend, a hopeful dream.
Crickets hum a soothing tune,
Underneath the silver moon.

Ethereal whispers linger near,
Carried softly for all to hear.
In nature's arms, I find my rest,
In waters deep, my soul is blessed.

Secrets Held in Smoky Stillness

In shadows thick, where silence sleeps,
Ancient tales the forest keeps.
Through wisps of fog, the truth lies bare,
In smoky stillness, secrets share.

Time weaves through trees, both wise and bold,
Whispering stories, ages old.
Each breath of mist, a voice profound,
In this quiet, the lost are found.

Moonlight filters through the haze,
Guiding souls through nature's maze.
The air thick with dreams deferred,
In stillness, I seek the unheard.

Footfalls soft on dampened ground,
In this peace, my heart is found.
Nature holds her breath, it seems,
As I wander through my dreams.

Secrets weave in silver threads,
Amongst the roots where silence spreads.
Embraced by stillness, deeply I dwell,
In the beauty of the unspoken spell.

Shifting Haze in Nature's Reverie

In morning's light, the shadows shift,
Nature's canvas, a subtle gift.
Through golden rays, the fog will fade,
Revealing wonders softly made.

Mountains loom in shifting scenes,
Awakening the forest dreams.
Every breath, a whispered sigh,
As colors dance against the sky.

Petals tremble in the breeze,
Nature sways with graceful ease.
In the haze, the world transforms,
In gentle swirls, new beauty warms.

A symphony of sounds resound,
In this reverie, peace is found.
The rhythm of life sings through the air,
In every moment, a loving care.

With each step upon the ground,
In shifting haze, I'm truly found.
Nature's heart beats in my chest,
In this dance, I find my rest.

Whispers from the Foggy Depths

In twilight's cloak, the fog descends,
A shroud of dreams where silence bends.
Whispers float on the chilly breeze,
Carrying secrets among the trees.

Echoes of laughter, faint and near,
Memories linger, cherished and dear.
Through the mist, shadows softly sway,
As night embraces the fading day.

In the depths where shadows play,
Forgotten hopes will find their way.
Voices call from the dark embrace,
In this haven, I find my space.

Rippling waters kiss the shore,
In the hush, I long for more.
Each drop of dew, a tale unfolds,
In whispers timeless and bold.

As I wander lost in thought,
In foggy depths, wisdom is sought.
Nature speaks in soft refrains,
In the quiet, my spirit gains.

Flickering Shadows in the Twilight Realm

In twilight's breath, shadows play,
Dancing softly, fading away.
Whispers linger on the breeze,
Secrets held beneath the trees.

Stars awaken, a celestial sheet,
Silent echoes in night's heartbeat.
Moonlight spills on eager ground,
Where ancient dreams can still be found.

Glimmers flicker, a spectral dance,
Drawing eyes in a wistful trance.
Each shadow tells a tale untold,
Of forgotten moments, bold and old.

Night wraps tightly, a velvet shroud,
Veiling the world in a tranquil cloud.
With lingering sighs, the shadows wane,
As dawn approaches, breaking the chain.

In twilight's arms, all is serene,
Within the realm where few have been.
Flickering shadows weave their spell,
In the twilight realm, all is well.

Night's Caress on the Wistful Waters

The moon reflects on tranquil waves,
In night's embrace, the silence saves.
Ripples dance with gentle grace,
Whispers linger in this place.

Stars alight like scattered dreams,
Guiding hearts with silver beams.
The water sings a soft refrain,
Of love and loss, joy and pain.

Beneath the sky, two souls unite,
In shadow's glow, they find the light.
With every wave, they dare to tread,
On wistful waters, where dreams are fed.

The night is rich with secrets deep,
In the silence, they gently weep.
As tides whisper tales of old,
In hushed hallowed moments, bold and gold.

Caressed by night, the waters sigh,
Beneath the starlit, endless sky.
Where hope is born in every wave,
In night's caress, the heart feels brave.

Elysian Phantoms in the gloaming

In gloaming's light, the phantoms roam,
In ethereal grace, they find their home.
Whispers echo through the fields,
Where nature's magic softly yields.

Flashes of silver guide their path,
Tracing the edges of twilight's bath.
Each phantom dances, a fleeting glance,
In the air, a quiet trance.

Night's embrace holds a timeless song,
Where shadows gather, right or wrong.
In the fading light, they weave and spin,
Elysian phantoms, where dreams begin.

Ghostly laughter fills the air,
As stars awaken with gentle care.
In shimmering veils, they intertwine,
Casting spells, a force divine.

In twilight's arms, they dare to play,
Elusive spirits that softly sway.
In the gloaming, they find their breath,
Elysian phantoms, defying death.

Afterglow Beneath the Muffled Sky

Beneath a sky, so muted and grey,
The afterglow finds a gentle way.
Fading colors, a soft goodbye,
As twilight whispers its silent sigh.

The horizon melts into the night,
With shades of purple, out of sight.
Stars awaken, one by one,
In the embrace of a setting sun.

Time stands still in this sacred hour,
Where shadows breathe, and moments flower.
In the stillness, hearts beat slow,
As dreams unfurl in the afterglow.

Muffled whispers dance in the air,
Secrets linger, a tranquil affair.
Beneath the stars, all fears subside,
In the quiet, love will abide.

The afterglow wraps the world in light,
Guiding souls through the gentle night.
In this space, we find our way,
Beneath the sky, come what may.

Whispers in the Mist

Soft whispers float in evening's air,
Each breath a secret, a silent prayer.
The world fades away, cloaked in gray,
As shadows and dreams begin to play.

Flickers of light through the fog entwine,
Unseen voices weave stories divine.
Mysteries linger where silence reigns,
In the heart of the mist, wonder remains.

Ghostly figures glide, lost in the haze,
Echoing laughter from distant days.
A dance of illusions, ethereal and bright,
In the chambers of dusk, they take flight.

Time holds its breath, its passage unclear,
While whispers embrace what we hold dear.
Moments suspended in twilight's grace,
Among the soft shadows, we find our place.

Shadows Dance on Dusk's Canvas

On dusk's gentle canvas, shadows unite,
Silhouettes twirling in the fading light.
Whispers of colors blend softly and sigh,
As night drapes its cloak across the sky.

A ballet of twilight, each figure serene,
Brushstrokes of darkness, vivid and keen.
The stars peek shyly, their sparkles faint,
As the moon starts to hum a silvered chant.

The earth holds its breath, the world slows its pace,
In the arms of evening, we find our place.
With each passing moment, dreams begin to prance,
Lost in the rhythm of shadows' dance.

Fleeting and ethereal, time sways in dusk,
Embracing the stillness, cradling the husk.
In this painted hush, we long to remain,
Where life turns to art, devoid of all pain.

Veils of Haze in Twilight's Embrace

Veils of haze drift, soft as a dream,
Wrapping the world in a silken seam.
Twilight unfolds, painting skies pale,
As whispers of sweetness begin to prevail.

The horizon blushes, shy and discreet,
With soft golden tones where day and night meet.
In this tender light, hopes gently sway,
As twilight's embrace ushers night into play.

Beneath the vast sky, we feel the sigh,
Of mysteries hidden as moments fly by.
In the heart of the dusk, we breathe and we feel,
The magic that wraps us, hidden yet real.

A tapestry woven with stars and with dreams,
In the hush of the night, life's wonder redeems.
Veils of haze linger, soft as a breath,
In twilight's embrace, we dance with our depths.

Luminous Reflections on Misted Waters

Luminous reflections dance on the lake,
Guided by whispers of ripples that break.
Stars spill their secrets, shimmering bright,
In the cradle of water, embraced by the night.

Each shimmer a story, a long-forgotten tale,
Woven with dreams on a silken sail.
Nature's soft canvas, where colors entwine,
Drawing us closer to that sacred line.

Faint echoes of laughter float on the breeze,
As shadows and moonlight unite with ease.
Reflections of moments, both tender and sweet,
In the arms of the water, our hearts skip a beat.

Golden horizons fade into dusk,
Wrapped in the magic, an ember of trust.
Luminous allure calls us to stay,
In misted waters, we find our way.

9 781805 595908